THE JODRELL BANK RADIO TELESCOPE

A recent invention, this famous telescope is used not only for tracking artificial satellites and space missiles, but was originally intended for exploring, and increasing our knowledge of, the Universe.

The great reflecting bowl—designed to funnel radio signals from outer space into the tiny central aerial—is 250 feet in diameter.

Series 601

Here is a book for children who want to know "How, why, where and when?"

It tells about some of the great inventions which have helped to make the modern world. The stories are simple and clear, and start with the invention of the printing press and end with the dawn of the atomic age. There is an exciting and colourful picture by Robert Ayton on every opening.

GREAT INVENTIONS

by RICHARD BOWOOD
with illustrations by ROBERT AYTON

Ladybird Books Loughborough

The Printing Press

This book is printed. Thousands of children have a copy, and the words and pictures in each are exactly the same. But there was a time when every book had to be written by hand and every picture drawn and painted. If you think for a moment, you will understand what a tremendous difference the invention of printing has made to the world.

Printing was invented by a German, Johann Gutenberg, who printed the Bible in 1456. They knew about printing a thousand years ago in China, but before Gutenberg it was only done by cutting out all the letters on a page on one block of wood. Quick printing began when Gutenberg had the idea of cutting letters on small blocks of metal which could be used again and again, fitted into a frame. This is called *movable type*.

The art of printing spread quickly. The first English printer was William Caxton, who set up his printing press in Westminster in 1476. Caxton was the first to print books in his own language. Before him all printed books had been in Latin. Caxton translated foreign books into English and he also printed the books of English authors, including the great poet Chaucer, and so helped to form the English language. In fifteen years Caxton printed more than a hundred different books.

Caxton and his printing press

0 7214 0132 5

The Telescope

When the Italian Galileo was a boy his parents did not know whether he would be a musician, an artist, or a scientist, for he was clever at everything. He had an enquiring mind; he always wanted to know *how* and *why*, and he became one of the great scientists of the world.

He was Professor of Mathematics at Padua University in 1609 when he heard about a wonderful invention made in Holland. It was a tube with two lenses in it, and when you looked through the tube objects seemed to be nearer and larger. Galileo did not see one of these instruments, but he at once began thinking about the idea and he made one for himself. When he looked through it things seemed to be three times as close.

The new invention was called the *telescope*, from the Greek words *far* and *to see*. Galileo devoted his time and his great scientific knowledge to making stronger ones. He learned how to grind and polish glass to make lenses, and he worked hard until he made telescopes which magnified eight times, and eventually thirty-three times.

Galileo was richly rewarded for his work by his government, and his powerful telescopes were eagerly bought all over Europe. He used his telescope to study the heavens and he discovered the mountains on the moon, the spots on the sun, the satellites of Jupiter, and showed that the Milky Way was a collection of millions of stars.

Galileo and his telescope

The Sextant and the Chronometer

If you were at sea on a long voyage, far from sight of land, how would you find out exactly where you were? Sailors could only work out their position roughly until an Englishman, John Hedley, made an important invention in 1731. This was the *sextant*, an instrument with which a sailor could tell his position by observing the angle of the sun or a star above the horizon, and then making a calculation from a book of tables.

John Hedley's invention was very important, but something else was wanted. To find out the exact position the sailor had to know the exact time in *England*. Time changes as you travel round the world and no clock or watch was accurate enough. A very special kind of watch was needed.

The problem was solved by another Englishman, John Harrison. He spent many years making a very accurate watch, called a *chronometer*. In 1761 he sent his son on a six weeks' voyage to test his fourth watch. When he arrived in Jamaica the watch was only 5 seconds wrong. Harrison was awarded a prize of £20,000 by the Government. With a chronometer to tell the true Greenwich time, seamen could use the sextant to work out their exact position at sea.

Finding a ship's position in the days of sail

Spinning and Weaving

Have you ever thought that cotton is made from fluffy plants, and wool from the coats of sheep? For thousands of years mankind has made thread for weaving into cloth from short pieces of wool, flax, cotton and other things, teased apart and spun together into thread.

Spinning was always done by hand with a spinning wheel until, in 1764, a Lancashire weaver named James Hargreaves made a famous invention. The legend is that he thought of it when he knocked over his wife's spinning wheel and saw the wheel spin round. His idea was to make a machine which would spin several threads at once. He worked hard at the problem and made a machine which spun eight threads, and then twenty-six. It was called the spinning-jenny.

Three other inventions followed within twenty years which together were to make Britain a great industrial country. Four years after Hargreaves invented this spinning-jenny, Sir Richard Arkwright made a spinning machine driven by power, first by a horse and then by a water-wheel. The two inventions were combined by Samuel Crompton in a machine called the spinning-mule.

The fourth invention was made by the Reverend Edmund Cartwright in 1785. This was the power loom. Until then cloth was woven on hand looms, but Cartwright invented a way to do it with machinery. Factories were built and the new machines installed. Britain sold cloth to foreign countries and soon became the richest country in the world.

10

The Steam Engine

One day, in 1763, a young Scotsman named James Watt began to mend a model engine. It was a model of a steam engine which had been invented sixty years before, and was used to pump water out of coal mines. As James Watt mended the model he made a great decision—he would try to invent a better kind of steam engine.

He studied steam and made many experiments, and at last he built his first full-size steam engine. To his joy it worked, and produced more power for its size than the old type, and used less fuel. Watt devoted all his time and energy to steam engines, and went into partnership with a Birmingham manufacturer, Matthew Boulton. Soon Boulton and Watt became famous for their engines.

Good though their steam engines were, they only drove a shaft backwards and forwards, for pumping. Then Watt made his second and very important invention. It was a great day when he patented it in 1781. The new idea was a steam engine which drove a wheel round.

It gave the world a new source of power. Steam engines could be used to drive wheels—the wheels of locomotives, the paddles of ships, the machinery in factories. It was the beginning of a new age—*the Age of Steam*, which led to Britain becoming a great manufacturing nation.

James Watt and an early steam engine

The Railway Engine

George Stephenson's father was a stoker of a colliery engine near Newcastle-upon-Tyne. When George was fourteen he became his father's assistant at a shilling a day. He loved engines and spent all his spare time studying them. That was in 1795, and in those days all steam engines were stationary. They were used to haul trucks along rails with a chain or rope.

In 1804 a Cornishman, Richard Trevithick, built an engine on wheels, and several other engineers built locomotives, as they were called, each one trying to make a better one than the others. George Stephenson set himself to build a locomotive.

Stephenson built his first locomotive in 1814, and he kept on trying to improve it. When the first public railway was opened between Stockton and Darlington in 1825 it was his engine, called *Locomotion*, which hauled the first goods train in the world, with a few passengers on board.

Stephenson's most famous engine was *The Rocket*, which his son Robert helped to design. In 1829 a prize of £500 was offered to the designer of the best locomotive. Five engines took part in the tests and *The Rocket* proved to be the best in every way. It astonished everyone by hauling a train at the wonderful speed of 30 miles an hour. With Robert, George Stephenson became the leading railway engineer in the world, both for building engines and making railways. Engines had jolly names in those days, and one very famous one was called *Puffing Billy*.

George Stephensons "Rocket," 1829

The Steamship

When James Watt perfected the steam engine men naturally turned their thoughts to using it for ships. One of the earliest successful steamships was built by an American, Robert Fulton, in 1807. She was called *Clermont* and she was driven with paddle-wheels on each side, but she had masts and sails as well. Her first voyage was up the Hudson River from New York to Albany, and her average speed was just over four-and-a-half miles an hour.

Sailors were naturally scornful of a ship driven by a steam engine. Sailing ships were graceful and, with a good wind, they were fast. The early steamships were neither graceful nor fast, but the men who believed in them persevered.

The first ship to cross the Atlantic entirely under steam was the *Sirius*, in 1838. More and more steamships were built, all with paddle-wheels, and with masts, so that they could use their sails as well. In 1840 the Cunard Company built four steamships for a regular service to America.

The sailors who had mocked at the idea of engines in ships were even more scornful when it was known that an iron steamship was being built. Everyone knew that wood floats and iron sinks, but the new iron ships *did* float, and in 1844 the *Great Britain* was launched at Bristol. She was the largest ship in the world and was built of iron. Instead of paddle-wheels she was driven by a screw. She still had sails, with six masts. It was the *Great Britain* which proved that the day of the steamship had come.

An early steamship with paddle-wheels

The Steam Turbine

The steam engine uses the force of steam to drive a piston in a cylinder. The force of steam is used in another type of engine—the steam turbine. The basic idea is quite simple. It is rather like a windmill, where the wind blows on the vanes and turns them round, to drive a shaft. In the steam turbine, jets of steam expand between the vanes on a shaft and those on the casing, and spin it round, providing smooth and constant power.

The inventor was Sir Charles Parsons. After studying at Cambridge University he joined an engineering firm and devoted his time to inventing the steam turbine. As with so many other new ideas it had been studied by others, but without success. Parsons refused to be discouraged by failures, and in 1884 his perseverance was rewarded; he made a steam turbine which worked.

The idea was improved by Parsons and other engineers and the machines were perfected. In 1890 steam turbines began to be installed in electric power stations. A turbine was fitted to a ship in 1897, and when it was tested it was proved that the turbine drove the ship faster than a steam engine. In 1907 two great new British liners, the *Lusitania* and the *Mauritania* were built with steam turbines. Now turbines are used in all large ships, and they also provide the power to drive the dynamos in electric power stations.

The turbines of a modern ship

The Davy Safety Lamp

When coal miners are working deep underground there is a great danger of disaster if a gas called firedamp is allowed to collect in the narrow galleries. If a naked flame or a spark comes into contact with a concentration of firedamp it can explode. To-day mines are scientifically ventilated and equipped with electric light, but even with these precautions terrible accidents occur.

In the old days they tried all manner of methods to give a coal mine light without risking an explosion. They even tried using a bowl of decaying fish, so that the miner could see from the faint phosphorescence given off by the fish skins. They tried to bring daylight down into the mine by using mirrors, as reflectors. Another idea was a steel wheel rotating against flint, to send off a shower of sparks.

The problem was solved in 1815 by Sir Humphry Davy. He was not connected with coal-mining, but he was a very clever chemist. He had started life as a surgeon's apprentice in Penzance, and by his hard work and brilliant brain he rose to become a Fellow of the Royal Society, and he was knighted for his discoveries.

Sir Humphry Davy's invention was simple. He designed an oil lamp with a fine gauze round the flame, so that the heat was prevented by the gauze from getting out to ignite dangerous firedamp. It was called the Davy Safety lamp and until electric lighting was introduced into coal mines it was always used. It prevented accidents and saved countless lives.

Old-time coal miner with a Davy safety lamp

The Sewing Machine

Imagine that you are watching your mother sewing carefully by hand, and that you have the idea of inventing a machine for sewing. How would you set about it? If you watch a modern sewing machine and see how fast the needle flashes up and down, and how fast and even the sewing comes out, you realise what a lot of thinking the inventors had to do.

In 1790 an Englishman patented the idea for a sewing machine, but it was never made. No-one knew anything about it until 100 years later. Meanwhile, in 1830, a Frenchman, Thimonnier, invented a sewing machine which worked. It was made mainly of wood. Thimonnier was a poor man, and he won neither fame nor fortune in his life; indeed he was nearly murdered. In 1840 eighty of his machines were being used in Paris to make army uniforms, when an ignorant mob attacked the place. They thought that the machines would put them out of work, so they smashed them all and attacked the unfortunate inventor as well.

Many other inventors were working on the problem, and about 1832 an American named Elias Howe had a brilliant idea. He devised a needle with the eye at the pointed instead of at the blunt end and that made all the difference to sewing machines. A great number of patents were taken out in the years that followed, as one inventor after another thought of improvements, and so the modern sewing machine came into being. Think of the time that invention has saved.

The Paris mob wrecking the first sewing machines

Electricity

Man has known of the existence of a mysterious force called electricity since ancient days; there is even a mention of it in the year 600 B.C. But it is only in the past hundred-and-fifty years that we have discovered how to use electricity. The first important discoveries were made by an Italian scientist Volta. In 1800 he made batteries, which gave out electricity. But it was a British scientist, Michael Faraday, who made the greatest discoveries.

Faraday was the son of a Yorkshire blacksmith who moved to London, where young Michael began his working life as errand boy to a bookbinder. But his one interest was science and in 1812, when he was twenty-one, he wrote to the famous Sir Humphry Davy and was made his assistant. He was so successful that when Sir Humphry died, Faraday succeeded him as Professor at the Royal Institution.

Faraday made a number of important discoveries in chemistry, but his greatest work was on electricity. He studied the work of previous scientists and spent twenty years experimenting to find out how to *make* electricity.

It was in 1831 that he had his greatest success. With simple apparatus, consisting of a magnet, a copper disc, and wire, he made, or *induced* an electric current. It meant that this magic force could at last be produced at will. It was the beginning of the dynamo, or electric generator, which produces the electricity used for power and light throughout the modern world.

Faraday in his laboratory

Electric Light

Michael Faraday discovered how to make electricity by mechanical means, and he and other scientists developed the dynamo, which provided electric current to drive machines. But electricity was not used for lighting until fifty years afterwards.

Two men made the discovery of how to use electricity for light at about the same time. One was an Englishman and the other an American. The Englishman was Sir Joseph Swan, an electrical engineer and chemist, who studied the problem for twenty years before he hit upon the solution. The American was the famous inventor Thomas Edison, who made a number of important inventions.

Both Swan and Edison discovered in different ways that if a current of electricity is passed through a fine thread or filament of carbon, it will glow white hot and give a strong light. The thread of carbon was enclosed in a glass bulb from which the air had been extracted, making a vacuum.

During the following years better materials were discovered for the filament and manufacturers found out how to make electric light bulbs quickly and cheaply. Power stations were built in towns to supply the electricity, where the great machines hum as they send the current by cable and wire to nearly every home in the land. By the touch of a switch we can have light or heat or power.

The generating room of an electric power station

The Telephone

One of the uses of electricity was to send messages along a wire. In various ways the receiver could read the letters or words, and messages could be sent over long distances. When cables were laid under the oceans, messages could be sent to a person living thousands of miles away.

This was a wonderful improvement on the old methods, when a letter had to be taken by a rider on horseback, mail coach, train, or ship. There was a better method still waiting to be discovered, however —the *telephone*.

The inventor of the telephone was a Scotsman, Alexander Graham Bell. He was educated at Edinburgh University. He went to Canada when he was a young man and then to America. He set himself to solve the problem of making an apparatus for speaking, by which two people could converse at a distance connected by wire. The first sound he transmitted was the twanging of a clock spring, and in 1876 he had the thrill of speaking to his assistant in the next room. The telephone was invented.

Other people had been working on the invention before Bell, but his was the first really efficient apparatus. He quickly improved it and, gradually at first, people took to the idea until the telephone became an essential part of everyday life.

Graham Bell experimenting with his telephone

Wireless Telegraphy

It was a Scotsman, Clerk Maxwell, who made wireless possible. He was a mathematician, and in 1863 he worked out, entirely by mathematics, that wireless communication must be possible. The next step was taken twenty-five years later when a German, Heinrich Hertz, made experiments which proved that Maxwell's theory was true.

Other scientists worked on the problem, and in 1896 Guglielmo Marconi, a twenty-two-year-old Italian, discovered how to send signals by wireless. He made many experiments and in 1901 he succeeded in sending signals across the Atlantic to America.

This wonderful invention was quickly adopted, especially at sea. Ships could send and receive messages and were ever ready in an emergency to send the distress signal—S.O.S.

The next problem was to transmit the human voice by wireless. Clever men all over the world made countless experiments and gradually the problems were solved. The most important part of the invention was the wireless valve. Transmitters and receivers were improved and it became possible to transmit the human voice, music and any sounds. Wireless telephony, which we now call radio, was invented.

Wireless at sea.   A wireless operator sending "S.O.S."

The Bicycle

The bicycle first became known as a means of transport when the 'hobby horse' was shown at an exhibition in Paris in 1818. It was a wooden frame with two wooden wheels and no pedals, and the rider pushed himself along with his feet on the ground.

It was in 1839 that the first real bicycle came into being. A Scottish blacksmith fitted his hobby-horse with pedals, rather like stirrups. He rode it for many years and was once prosecuted for furious riding.

The next important development was the French Velocipede. It had the front wheel slightly larger than the back one, with pedals on the front hub. It could not have been very comfortable because it was called a 'Boneshaker'; but it was very popular, especially in Britain.

After the Boneshaker came the 'Penny-Farthing', so called because the front wheel was much larger than the back. An important feature was the use of steel wheels instead of wood, and solid rubber tyres.

The modern bicycle began with the 'Safety' bicycle, which had pedals and chain as now. The first of this type was made in France, but the best early model was Lawson's of 1873. When the safety bicycle was given pneumatic tyres, ball-bearings, a free-wheel, and better brakes, it became the bicycle we ride to-day.

A Boneshaker and a Penny-Farthing

The Pneumatic Tyre

It was a thrill for children in the old days to watch an iron rim fitted to a wooden wheel. The rim was made just too small for the wheel and then it was made red hot, so that it would expand. It was dropped over the wheel and hammered on while it was red-hot, and then water was thrown over it. With a great sizzling noise and a lot of steam the iron rim contracted to its proper size—and was firmly fitted to the wheel.

All wheels had iron rims, except on expensive carriages and bicycles with solid rubber tyres, until 1888. Then a Belfast veterinary surgeon named John Dunlop had an idea. He used to drive round to visit farmers in a dog-cart, and the iron rims made a lot of noise and were uncomfortable on the rough roads. "Would it not be possible", he thought, "to make tyres of rubber tubes filled with air?"

Dunlop made a wooden disc, nailed a rubber tube on to it, filled it with air and covered it with a strip of linen. He took it into his back yard and removed the front wheel off his son's tricycle.

First he rolled the tricycle wheel across the yard. It went a little way and then toppled over. Then Dunlop rolled his wheel with the new tyre. It went right across the yard and bounced against the wall. It was the proof he wanted. The next year he formed a company to make pneumatic tyres.

Dunlop demonstrating a pneumatic bicycle tyre

The Internal Combustion Engine and the Motor Car

The first motor car of all was made in 1875 by an Austrian, Siegfried Marcus. He used the *internal combustion engine*, which was gradually being perfected. But Marcus did not make cars to sell, and it is a German, Carl Benz, who is recognised as the father of the motor car. Benz made motor cars for sale in 1885, and with another German, Gottlieb Daimler, became the pioneers of the motor industry.

Engineers in many countries designed engines and motor cars. The earliest ones were built like horse carriages, and an early British company was called *The Great Horseless Carriage Company*. They looked like carriages, with large wheels and engines underneath the floor-boards.

Motor cars of all shapes and sizes were built and improvements were quickly made. The most famous was a British make. In 1906 a well-known sportsman, the Honourable Charles Rolls went into partnership with Henry Royce, an engineer. Together they built the Rolls-Royce motor car, which has long been known as the best car in the world.

Few inventions have made such a tremendous difference to everyday life as the internal combustion engine. It has altered the way of life with motor cars and motor cycles, buses, lorries and aeroplanes.

An early motor car

The Diesel Engine

While Daimler, Benz, and others were working on the internal combustion engine to drive their motor cars, others were trying to develop a different kind of engine. In the petrol engine the compressed petrol gas is exploded by a spark and drives the piston in the cylinder. In the other kind of engine, air is compressed in the cylinder, becomes very hot and when fuel oil is injected into it, it explodes—without a spark to set it off.

The first engine of this kind was devised by an Englishman, H. Akroyd Stuart, in 1890. A German, Rudolf Diesel, was also working on the same idea, and although his invention was not patented until two years after Stuart's, the engines are named after him.

Diesel had many disappointments, and once was nearly killed when an engine blew up. But in 1898 the Diesel engine was shown in an exhibition in Munich and was soon taken into general use.

It proved to be ideal for ships and boats, heavy lorries and motor buses. It was also used for railways, and very powerful Diesel engines are now gradually taking the place of the steam locomotive.

A modern Diesel locomotive

The Aeroplane

Man has always envied the birds, and for centuries scientists had tried to find out how to fly. It was not until the invention of the internal combustion engine, however, that flight in heavier than air machines became a practical possibility. Many people took part in the quest for the secret of flight and in 1903 two American brothers first flew in an aeroplane.

Orville and Wilbur Wright were partners in a bicycle repair business and began to make and fly gliders in 1900. In due course they modified a motor car engine to drive a propeller and fitted it to a specially adapted biplane glider. They first flew their aeroplane on December 17th, 1903, a great day in history. They made two flights each, the first of twelve seconds, the second and third longer, and the fourth lasted nearly a minute, which covered 852 feet. They kept on improving their machines until in 1908 Wilbur flew for an hour and twenty minutes.

Other enthusiasts made use of the knowledge gained by the first flights, and aeroplanes were made and flown in England, France, and America. In 1909 a Frenchman, Louis Bleriot, made history by flying the English Channel from Calais to Dover. With the outbreak of war in 1914 a great impetus was given to flying, and the aeroplanes of 1918 were much in advance of the flimsy machines of 1914.

A British warplane of 1914

The Jet Engine

For the first forty years aeroplanes were powered by internal combustion engines, which drove the propellers. In 1928 a young R.A.F. cadet, Frank Whittle, began to work out a new way of powering aeroplanes. It was to do away with propellers and to fly the aeroplane much faster with a jet engine. He worked at his idea, and when he was an officer and studying at Cambridge, in 1935, he patented his invention of the jet engine.

The jet engine works on the same principle as a rocket. Air is drawn into the front of the engine and is burned with paraffin. The gas so formed expands violently and rushes out of the back of the engine—in a jet, and propels the aeroplane forward with great power.

Other engineers were working on the same idea, especially in Germany and Italy, but Whittle did not know this. He formed a company to make jet engines, but no-one took much notice until war broke out in 1939. That made all the difference. The Government took up the idea and the jet engine was developed urgently. Before the end of the war fighters were flying at high speeds, powered by jet engines.

After the war jet engines were developed further. Jet powered aeroplanes have flown at more than fifteen hundred miles an hour, and giant jet engined air-liners fly at speeds never dreamt of by the pioneers of flying fifty years ago.

A jet plane at speed

The Camera

Perhaps you have a camera; you will certainly have had your photograph taken and wondered at the magic of the camera. Many people had a hand in inventing photography, but the credit is given to an Englishman, William Fox Talbot. He took a photograph in 1835. Many other inventors worked at the idea, and the most important was the Frenchman, Daguerre.

Fox Talbot spread the chemicals for the pictures on paper. Daguerre went one better by using copper plates covered with silver. In 1851 glass plates were used for the first time, and in 1884 film was made of celluloid.

The next development was the moving picture, and here again a number of people were concerned. An Englishman, William Friese-Greene, is recognised as the father of the moving picture, though important work was done by an American, Edison, and a Frenchman, Lumiere.

For moving pictures a long strip of celluloid is used, which unwinds inside the camera while the shutter opens and shuts rapidly. The series of pictures shown through a projector shows the movement.

The first public showing of a film was in London in 1890. Many improvements were made by inventors, mostly in America. At first only very short films were made, but in 1903 a complete exciting story was filmed. So gradually, the cinema industry was born.

Making a film

Television

In 1922 a Scotsman, named John Logie Baird, assembled some rather odd apparatus in his bedroom in a Hastings lodging house. He had his wash-stand for his work bench, a tea chest, an electric motor from a junk shop, two lenses from cycle lamps, a torch, parts of a dismantled army radio and some wire. He also had string, glue and sealing wax.

Baird had gone to live in Hastings because he was ill. He was poor and he had no job. Yet he had set himself the task of inventing an apparatus which would send pictures by radio—*television*. It was a problem many people were trying to solve. Baird was not daunted by his many handicaps, and he persevered stubbornly with his meagre materials. For two years he had no success, but he kept at it, and at last he was rewarded. One day he transmitted the picture of a Maltese Cross over a distance of three yards.

He moved to London, and after overcoming many difficulties, he had another success—he transmitted the image of a boy's head from the camera in one room to the receiver in another. A few months later members of the Royal Institution went to see the invention and it was proved to be a complete success.

On September 30th, 1929, the B.B.C. gave its first television broadcast, using Baird's system. Seven years later they changed to another system. But the young Scotsman in the Hastings boarding house had achieved his dream, and he is honoured in Britain as *the Father of Television*.

A television unit at work

Radar

If you shout at a high wall a short distance away your voice sometimes comes back to you as an echo, because the sound waves are reflected off the wall. That is the principle of Radar, but instead of sound waves it is radio waves which are reflected. The discovery was made a few years before the last war, when radio waves from a transmitting station were reflected back from a distant aeroplane.

It was realised that if an apparatus could be devised to send out radio waves all the time and record the echoes from any approaching aeroplanes, it would be a wonderful method of defence in war.

Scientists set about solving the problem and Radar was invented. Apparatus was made which sent out waves in pulses, and the presence of a distant aeroplane was shown on the screen of a cathode ray tube, which is what we have in a television set. It was all done in closest secrecy and Radar stations were built round the coast. Long before enemy aircraft reached our shores the Anti-Aircraft and the Fighter Squadrons were warned.

After the war Radar was put to peaceful uses. It was installed at airports to guide aeroplanes down safely in fog. It was fitted to ships so that they are warned of obstructions ahead, such as icebergs. It guides ships into port. It provides aeroplanes and ships with a magic eye, with which they can see far into the distance, in the dark or in fog.

The magic eye of Radar

Atomic Energy

At Calder Hall, in Cumbria, Britain built the first large atomic power station in the world. Atomic energy is obtained by splitting atoms of a rare metal, uranium, in apparatus called a reactor. The atom is the smallest form of matter. You would need several million atoms to cover the head of a pin, yet the whole world is made of atoms.

When atoms are split in a reactor they give off tremendous energy, and scientists have discovered how to control and use that energy. The atoms also give off highly dangerous radiation, so reactors are heavily shielded and the men operating them wear special protective clothing.

At an atomic power station the reactors get very hot, and the gas which is passed through them becomes very hot, too. This hot gas then passes into the boilers, where it makes steam to drive the turbines. In turn, the turbines drive the dynamos which make electricity. At Calder Hall one ton of uranium does the work of 10,160 tonnes of coal.

The electricity thus made is taken over wires to drive machinery in factories and to provide light and heat in houses. In another form atomic plant can be used to propel ships. It is a miraculous new source of power which heralds a new era—*the Atomic Age*.

Handling plutonium in an atomic research station

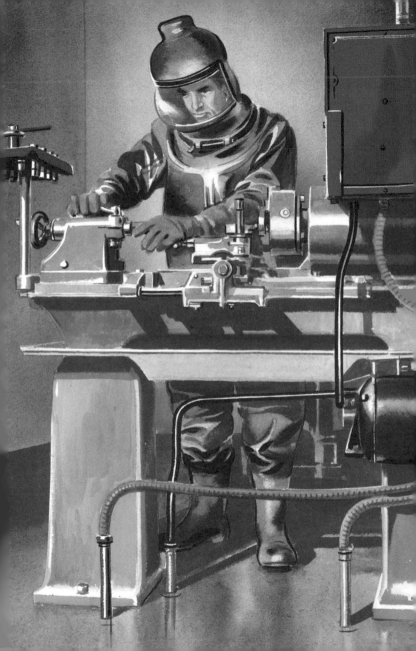